COMMUNISM

IN

PROPHECY

HISTORY

AMERICA

by Rev. Gerald B. Winrod, D. D.

Defender Publishers ... Wichita, Kansas

ISBN: 978-2-925369-40-0
Printed in the USA.

TABLE OF CONTENTS

~~~~~~~~~~~~~ CHAPTER ONE ~~~~~~~~~~~~~

Communism In The Apocalypse

WE SHALL TRACE three major lines of thought related to the menace of international Communism.

First . . . Consideration will be given to the subject in the light of prophetical Scripture. Inspiration writes with a legible hand. The prophecies of the Bible contain a message for the times in which we live. Prophecy is history written in advance.

The precision with which world trends are fitting into the moulds of Scripture answers critics who look upon this department of theological science as a meaningless diversion. The practical value of prophetic knowledge is demonstrated by current happenings among the nations. There is no rational explanation for present catastrophic changes except as we consult the inspired timetable.

Second . . . Consideration will be given to the subject in the light of historical research. A philosopher once said that to know a thing well, one must understand its first cause. Communism, now reaching fruition among the nations, is not of recent origin.

The roots of the conspiracy reach deep into eighteenth century history. I have traced it as a tangible organization back to the year 1776. Beyond that, the movement becomes somewhat nebulous as far as historical records are concerned. But we know it to be an age old attack upon the program and purposes of God for our humanity.

Third . . . Consideration will be given to the subject in the light of recent disclosures showing how the red scourge is threatening the free institutions of the United States. The White House did everything possible to encourage Communism during Franklin Roosevelt's administration.

The dislocation of America's religious, moral, economic and political structure does not result from natural disorders. Our plight came as the product of planning by international anti-christs who hate the Country that Christians love. The secret blueprint of the plot is now in the hands of patriotic Americans and this is spreading consternation among the conspirators.

Introducing the Characters

THE SIXTH CHAPTER of the book of Revelation was written for the times in which we live. The four horsemen and their steeds, portrayed in this passage, represent four great world principles. The horses are globe trotters, predicted to operate on an international scale.

John was an old man, residing on the isle of Patmos, at the time he saw the vision. He had been banished to this desolate spot in the Aegean Sea because of his loyalty to Christ and the Gospel.

The message was penned A. D. 95 to 97. Irenaeus said: "It was given not long ago, almost in our own generation, at the close of Domitian's reign."

Our word Revelation comes from the Greek "apocalypsis" and means "unveiling." The title suggests that far from being a sealed mystery, the book is to be studied and its contents mastered. This negates the idea that it is abstruse and beyond the range of human comprehension.

Special advantages are promised persons who devote time and effort to the book. We read in Revelation 1:3, "Blessed is he that readeth, and they that hear the words of this prophecy, and keep those things which are written therein: for the time is at hand."

The Revelation, considered as a whole, treats of the establishment of Christ's kingdom on earth in answer to the Lord's prayer. Most of the book is concerned with hardening judgments destined to break upon the world during the end time, just before the inauguration of the kingdom.

The final climax of horror is described in the twenty-fourth chapter of Matthew as the "great tribulation." The nations are rapidly sweeping into that period.

While the symbolic message of the four horsemen is identified with the closing scenes of the age, there is nothing to suggest that the steeds are confined to the tribulation period. Some teachers have even gone so far as to say that the white horse and rider cannot go forth until after the saints are translated.

The first horse to rise on the horizon and gallop across John's vision was white. "And I saw, and behold a white horse: and he that sat on him had a bow; and a crown was given unto him: and he went forth conquering, and to conquer."

The second horse was red. "And there went out another horse that was red: and power was given to him that sat thereon to take peace from the earth, and that they should kill one another: and there was given unto him a great sword."

The third horse was black. "And I beheld, and lo a black horse; and he that sat on him had a pair of balances in his hand. And I heard a voice in the midst of the four beasts say, A measure of wheat for a penny, and three measures of barley for a penny; and see thou hurt not the oil and the wine."

The fourth horse was pale (ashy green, the color of death). "And I looked, and behold a pale horse: and his name that sat on him was Death, and Hell followed with him. And power was given unto them over the fourth part of the earth, to kill with the sword, and with hunger, and with death, and with the beasts of the earth."

The terrors of tribulation that follow the appearance of these horses and their riders suggests the use of atomic energy for destructive purposes. "There was a great earthquake; and the sun became black as sackcloth of hair, and the moon became as blood; . . . And the heaven departed as a scroll when it is rolled together; and every mountain and island were moved out of their places."

Christ's faithful followers are scheduled to endure great

persecution during the time that these horses are galloping to and fro in the earth, because martyred saints of that period are quoted as crying: "How long, O Lord, holy and true, dost thou not judge and avenge our blood on them that dwell on the earth?"

The White Horse

E RRONEOUS INTERPRETATIONS of prophetical passages sometimes creep into the writings of well-meaning Bible students. Such errors, if repeated by others who fail to exercise originality of thought, frequently do great harm. False statements repeated again and again may be accepted as truth.

This is noted in the parrot-like repetitions of certain writers who insist upon circulating the fiction that the white horse and rider represent the rise of Antichrist. Unwittingly, some such published statements border upon blasphemy.

One teacher, for instance, makes the following bold statement, in a book recently released from the press: "The rider upon the white horse is the Antichrist, the false messiah." Another writer, obviously repeating what he had heard some one else say without giving the matter serious thought, remarks: "Because of the white horse, here mentioned, some have thought that this rider with the bow refers to the going forth of Christ through the Gospel message. Such a view is entirely incorrect."

In contrast, Bible students concerned with the task of placing these four symbols in their proper prophetical settings, will do well to weigh what Dr. William R. Newell says on the subject. Turning to page 102 of his treatise on the Apocalypse, we read:

"The white horse and rider are plainly connected with the holy hosts and armies that are in heaven. Heaven is no longer engaged in grace but in judgment. White Horse — this is holiness in exhibition and in warfare, for thus do white horses appear in Scripture. The rider has a bow, the weapon of long distance conflict.

"The Lord and the heavenly host are not yet coming (for the rider symbolizes not only Christ but the whole heavenly host now exhibited as antagonistic to earth). 'Thine arrows are sharp in the heart of the king's enemies,' is written in Psalm 45:5 of our Lord's coming.

" 'And there was given unto him a crown' denotes the fact that the Lord and the powers of heaven are to take the Kingdom away from men, and rule for God. 'He came forth conquering, and to conquer.' Some have amazingly conceived this white horse to represent the Antichrist!

"Not only would this be ABSOLUTELY OUT OF TIME (for the career of the Antichrist constitutes a woe under the seventh trumpet of the seventh seal) but how impossible to conceive of the Antichrist as conquering and to conquer— that is, to get the FINAL victory. This is what the phrase, 'conquering and to conquer' means—to achieve final and decisive conquest.

"And only Christ will ever do that."

Let those who subscribe to the untenable view that the

rider of the white horse is Antichrist, cite a single instance in Scripture where the color white symbolizes evil. On the contrary, Daniel specifically states that "in the latter times," when the transgressors are come to the full, a King of Fierce Countenance will stand up who understands "dark sentences." Black is the consistent color of Antichrist, not white.

It is a mistake to suppose that horses are always associated with evil in Scripture. Any such idea is refuted by the experience of Elisha's servant, concerning whom we read: "And the Lord opened the eyes of the young man; and he saw: and behold, the mountain was full of horses and chariots of fire round about Elisha."

The rider of the white horse is described as carrying "a bow." This is an instrument of warfare, but since no bloodshed connects with the rider, the effect must be moral rather than physical. Inspiration employs exactly the same imagery when explaining, in Habakkuk 3:8-9, the results that accompany conquests of salvation: "Thou didst ride upon thine horses and thy chariots of salvation. Thy bow was made quite naked, even thy word."

The white horse must be carefully placed in its proper relation to the calendar of end time events, in order to accurately decipher the message of the other three. If one holds to the mistaken idea that the steeds are confined to the tribulation period, he will derive no benefit from the teaching as it applies to the hour in which we live.

The interpretation of Dr. J. A. Seiss may well be added to that of Dr. William R. Newell, previously quoted. In his published Lectures on the Apocalypse, Dr. Seiss says:

"The color of the White Horse is the color of righteousness, triumph, peace. The picture must then somehow link itself with something righteous and good, though associated with a judicial proceeding.

"The language employed concerning the career of this horseman, is suggestive. He goes forth 'conquering, and to conquer.' There is an idea of continuity in the expression. It describes an ongoing of the work. It is not a past, or mere present success, but a continuous one, resulting, along with what else comes upon the scene, in complete and sovereign dominion.

"We are therefore authorized to expect that when the great transactions of the coming judgment begin, and the Lord lays bare the literal truthfulness of his word by the marvelous demonstrations then to be made, there will be a conquering of the hearts of men to the sovereignty of Heaven, such as has never been. And this is the sort of conquest and triumph which is set forth by the white horse, and his crowned rider, going forth conquering, and to conquer. It is the bloodless conquest of men to God, by the potencies of a present judgment.

"It is the knock of Christ at the door of the Church of the lukewarm Laodiceans—the sharp knock of terrifying judgment — in which He makes His last proposal to them, even of so much as to share of his supper."

The Jamieson, Fausset and Brown Commentary interprets the white horse as, "Evidently Christ. whether in person.

or by His angel, preparatory to His coming again. Crown, from the Greek 'stephanos,' means the garland or wreath of a conqueror, which is also implied by His white horse, white being the emblem of victory.

"In Revelation 9:11-12 the last step of His victorious progress is represented. Accordingly, there He wears many diadems and is personally attended by the hosts of heaven.

"The white horse of Christ's bloodless victories is soon followed by the red horse of bloodshed; but this is overruled to the clearing away of the obstacles of Christ's coming kingdom."

The Red Horse

PRIOR TO THE RISE of the Communist movement in its modern form, commentators lacked the wealth of information now available for interpreting the meaning of the red horse symbol. They could only deal in general terms, as for instance, the terse remark of Dr. G. B. M. Clouser: "The red horse with his rider, who has power to take peace from the earth—these speak of war, such as will characterize this period."

Jamieson, Fausset and Brown merely asserts that human blood will flow like a torrent when the red horse rides.

Dr. W. Lamb briefly states: "Fearful war will break out everywhere. In that terrible time there will be a world-wide reign of terror and bloodshed, and it is also then, that men will learn, to their cost, the terrible folly of ever imagining that peace is possible in a world that still rejects the Divine Christ."

Although recent writers on the Apocalypse are for the most part content to rehash these earlier generalities, detailed interpretations are now possible because the red horse clearly anticipates the development of red Communism in its world-wide ramifications.

The inspired record says that the red horse and rider will "take peace from the earth" and cause men to "kill one another."

Every peace gathering attempted since the close of the last war has been sabotaged by Soviet Russia. Delegates from other nations bring trowels to such conferences. But Moscow representatives prefer monkey wrenches, which they are adept at throwing into the peace machinery of the world.

Lunacharsky, Soviet Minister of Education, stated the official attitude of his government toward peace when he said: "What we want is hatred. We must know how to hate, for only thus shall we conquer the world."

Stalin said in a lecture before Sverdlov University in 1924: "One of the chief indirect reserves for the Communist revolution is antagonism, conflicts and wars."

On the evening of October 13, 1946, Louis F. Budenz delivered a radio address at Detroit in which he charged that Soviet Russia was feverishly preparing for a third world war. The reds were pictured as preparing to strike England and the United States at an unguarded moment, with the purpose in view of establishing a "world proletariat dictatorship."

Mr. Budenz, a former member of the Communist Party and editor of the Daily Worker, declared that members of the American organization were taking orders from a mystery man "who is an agent of the Kremlin" in this part of the world.

He continued: "When Russia feels able, the third world war will begin. I learned, at first very reluctantly, that Soviet Russia intends to destroy Britain and the United States. There is a man, an agent of the Kremlin, who directs all Communist activities in the United States.

"This man never shows his face. Communist leaders never see him, but they follow his orders and suggestions implicitly. The average Communist never heard of him."

The speaker volunteered to disclose the name of this agent of the Kremlin in the United States, preferably at a time and place when testimony could be given under oath. Thereupon, a New York newspaper published an interview with one Ruth Fischer, who stated that Mr. Budenz was referring to her brother, Gerhard Eisler, alias Hans Berger.

Miss Fischer was floor leader of the Communists in the German reichstag prior to the rise of the Nazis. She was later expelled from the Communist Party for some unexplained reason. Apparently estranged from her brother, she described him as "head of the Communists in the western hemisphere and one of the key figures in the American Communist Party."

Mr. Budenz admitted Eisler was the man, and stated that while serving as editor of the Daily Worker, he took orders secretly from him.

It later developed that Eisler, whose Jewish nationality is admitted, entered the United States by New Deal manipulation six years earlier, on a transit visa requiring his immediate departure for Mexico. He had been permitted to remain here. No move was made to leave until two days after the Budenz exposure. He was picked up by the Federal Bureau of Investigation trying to board a Russian ship. His second attempt was successful and he finally landed safely behind the iron curtain.

Soviet Russia will dare strike the United States only if assured that members of the red underground are organized to promote mob violence and weaken us internally.

The Congressional Committee on Un-American Activities sounded a needed warning in its 1946 Report to the Congress and the Nation. This legal body, of which Congressman John S. Wood was then chairman, says:

"The United States must fear Communism because it is a foreign-controlled totalitarian movement whose leaders in the past have openly proclaimed that it advocates revolution and the overthrow of the present government of the United States. Recent disavowals of this fact or these facts by the leaders of the Communist Party should not be given credence.

"Communists in the United States have for a long period of years put forth propaganda to the effect that they form only a small minority group. This is a shrewd maneuver on their part to divert attention from them while they infiltrate every phase of American life. It should be remembered that an insignificant minority group in Russia, numbering 200,000 persons, gained control of the Russian government, a country which had a population of 170,000,000. It is a fundamental part of Communist theory to hold party membership down to a minimum.

"A small minority group in time of war can effect the most damaging sabotage in any economic system. Before Hitler's attack on Stalinist Russia, the Communists in this country were engaged in nation-wide sabotage strikes against American military preparedness. For instance, the strike at North American Aviation in California is a good illustration of this point. The President of the United States was compelled to use the United States Army to put down that strike. He also asserted that Communists were firmly in control of the leadership of that strike which jeopardized the basic security of this country.

"If we had enough Communists in the United States Army, the Army would be of no value in a situation of this kind.

"Further, in speaking of the Communist doctrine of keeping the admitted membership in the party small, a statement of William Z. Foster on page 28 of his book entitled, 'The Russian Revolution,' says of the Communist Party, 'It is not a mass organization. Mere numbers mean nothing to it ... The masses would only clog up the organization machinery and prevent the smooth working of these militants. The Communist Party is the distilled essence of working class energy and revolutionary spirit. It is the little leaven that leaveneth the whole lump. Its influence and power is enormously greater than its small numbers would indicate'."

Red is the color of revolution. The red horse of the Apocalypse is galloping to and fro, dislocating the religious, moral, economic and political structure of the civilized world.

Brown Nazism sprang from the loins of the red beast of Bolshevism. Germany first turned to Communism and later produced Nazism. Both systems are totalitarian and therefore objectionable to Americans. The brown ideology is basically red.

Black Fascism sprang from the loins of the red beast of Bolshevism. Italy first turned to Communism and later produced Fascism. Both systems are objectionable for the reasons just stated. The black ideology is therefore basically red.

The Black Horse

THE THIRD HORSE of the Apocalypse anticipates world-wide food rationing. Only in the light of developments during the last few years does this prophecy become understandable.

While earlier writers were at a disadvantage, yet they succeeded in deciphering the meaning of this phase of the prophecy with remarkable accuracy. Rev. M. Baxter, writing in the year 1866, stated: "The judgment of war having been specifically inflicted during the second seal, there now follows the judgment of famine under the third seal. The black color of the horse is connected with the idea of famine, for in the fourth and fifth chapters of Lamentations that hue is described as characterizing people while suffering from dearth of food."

The venerable Baxter continued: "The balances in the hand of this equestrian upon the black horse also betoken food to have become so scarce as to require it to be carefully sold by weight, instead of by measure or size and quantity, and this delivery of food by weight is specified in the fourth chapter of Ezekiel to be the marked accompaniment of a predicted famine: 'Thy meat which thou shalt eat, shall be by weight, twenty shekels a day.' 'Moreover he said unto me, Son of man, behold, I will break the staff of bread in Jerusalem: and they shall eat bread by weight, and with care.'

"The voice from the, midst of the four living creatures still more distinctly proclaims this to be an unparalleled season of gaunt famine."

Baxter believed, and many modern Bible teachers concur, that the quantity of food mentioned in Revelation 6:5-6 is a one-day's supply per person. He said: "This measure of wheat which in the original Greek is called a 'choenix,' seems to have contained three or four cotylae, or modern half-pints; and, therefore, to have been equivalent to a pint and a half, a quart in our day, although writers on classical antiquities have experienced some difficulty in defining its exact size.

"It is also generally considered upon the authority of classical writers, that the 'choenix,' or measure, as it is here termed, was the usual moderate day's allowance of food to a soldier or slave; though a larger allowance might, without much difficulty, be consumed by one person if he could obtain it."

Dr. Clauser discusses this section of the prophecy succinctly: "The black horse speaks of the dark shadows of famine cast—of the pathetic conditions that always follow in the wake of war. War, famine and pestilence. These things are always related and inseparable."

Rigid rationing of food in many countries during and since the second world war, shows how the fulfillment of this prophecy is possible. The passage speaks of a time when there will be universal scarcity of edibles.

War and revolution destroy economic equilibrium, clog the wheels of agriculture and weaken transportation. But even more disconcerting is the fact that totalitarian systems use food control as a means for killing off large populations and subduing opposition.

The Bolsheviks were first to introduce the plan of requiring citizens to have food cards in order to live. One of their leaders is quoted as saying: "Food is a beautiful instrument for maneuvering and disciplining the masses."

Many believe that this was the real purpose behind the OPA, and other systems of control, shackled upon the American people by the administration of Franklin Roosevelt. Planned scarcity points the way to the era of the black horse. Famines, frequently produced by artificial methods, have taken a toll of human life numbering into the millions during the last three decades.

A member of the legislature in a certain middle State tells of spending two weeks in the Russian Ukraine nine years ago. He lived on raw fish and sunflower seed most of the time, despite the fact that his pockets were bulging with rubles. Huge bins were filled with grain, but food could not be purchased. Soldiers armed with fixed bayonets patrolled areas that he visited. Starving people who crossed lines drawn in the vicinity of the storage centers were put to death.

The nations have of late become famine minded. Food consumption is discussed in terms of calories.

Former President Hoover returned in May, 1946, from a trip around the world, serving in the capacity of "food ambassador," for President Truman. He made his report to the nation at a dinner in Chicago. Each guest was served a meal of six hundred calories consisting of the following foods: Thin soup containing three-fourths of an ounce of fats, one ounce of potatoes, one ounce of beets, one and four-fifths ounces of meat, the same portion of bread and a substitute for coffee.

Mr. Hoover delivered a highly informative address on food conditions throughout the world. His remarks were punctuated by several striking statements, such as the following:

"Hunger hangs over the homes of more than 800 million people—over one-third of the people of the earth. Hunger is a silent visitor who comes like a shadow. He sits beside every anxious mother three times a day. He brings not alone suffering and sorrow, but fear and terror. He carries disorder and the paralysis of government, and even its downfall. He is more destructive than armies, not only in human life, but in morals. All of the values of right living melt before his invasions, and every gain of civilization crumbles.

"Of the Four Horsemen of the Apocalypse, the one named war has gone—at least for a while. But famine, pestilence, and death are still charging over the earth. And the modern world has added four more to this evil brigade. Their names are destruction, drouth, fear and revolution. This crisis is not alone due to war destruction of agriculture. On the top of that calamity has been piled drouth in the Mediterranean, drouth in India, drouth in China, and partial drouth in South Africa and the Argentine. Never have so many evil horsemen come all at one time."

The Pale Horse

COMING TO THE FOURTH, or pale horse of the Apocalypse, and looking back upon the three previous steeds, one is impressed with the chain of events moving toward chaos.

The first horse anticipates righteous judgment, as suggested by arrows of truth aimed at the consciences and souls of men. The second depicts war, revolution and bloodshed. The third adds famine and starvation to the list. The fourth combines all the earlier horrors in such a way as to destroy one-fourth of the world's population and expand the borders of Hades to the earth plane.

The word pale in the passage means ashy or green,

the color most frequently associated with death. The description of the rider causes one to think of a hideous, grinning skeleton.

The tempo of judgment increases in proportion as human beings continue yielding to the Antichrist and his system of international control. The color ascribed to this period is indicative of the worst stages of human corruption. Unveiled as the personification of death and pestilence, the rider is accompanied by a companion from the place of departed spirits. The gates of Hades are opened so that excarnate beings gain access to the realm where humans live.

Only once before has anything of this nature occurred on our planet, namely, during the antediluvian period. The judgment of the deluge was the result. Jesus said: "As the days of Noah were, so shall also the coming of the Son of man be."

The Genesis record shows what happened to the early inhabitants of our earth who established unlawful relationship with excarnate beings. This fearful event served to accelerate the already rapid progress of evil. A similar state of affairs will come to exist when Death and Hades gallop to and fro on the pale horse.

The cause of the corruption that developed in antediluvian times is explained by Genesis 6:4, "There were giants in the earth in those days; and also after that, when the sons of God came in unto the daughters of men, and they bare children to them, the same became mighty men which were of old, men of renown."

Some have thought these words referred to intermarriage

between the descendents of Seth and Cain, but a careful examination of the passage will elicit a far deeper meaning. The first and second verses of this chapter explain that "men began to multiply and daughters were born unto them." This is followed by a reference to a second group, called "sons of God," entirely different from the race as a whole, described as "men."

The "sons of God" are plainly distinguished from the progeny of Adam. The term occurs four times in other parts of the Old Testament and refers, in each instance, to excarnate beings. Peter tells us that these daring rebels who left their estate and came to earth levels are now imprisoned criminals in "chains of darkness," to be reserved unto judgment."

A literal rendering of II Peter 2:4 would be as follows: "For if God spared not angels when they had sinned, but cast them down to Tartarus, and committed them to pits of darkness, to be reserved unto Judgment ... " Jude makes reference to these same disobedient creatures of damnation: "And the angels which kept not their first estate, but left their own habitation, he hath reserved in everlasting chains under darkness unto the judgment of the great day."

Dr. G. H. Pember believes that Genesis 6:4 should read as follows: "The Nephilim, or fallen ones, were on the earth in those days, and also afterwards, when the sons of God came in unto the daughters of men."

He also says: "Through a misapprehension of the Septuagint, the English version renders 'Nephilim' by 'giants.' But the form of the Hebrew word indicates a verbal adjective or noun, of passive or neuter signification from 'Napal,' to fall: hence it must mean 'the fallen ones,' that is, probably, the fallen angels.

"The meaning of 'giants,' in our sense of the term, is altogether secondary, and arose from the fact that those beings of mixed birth were said to have displayed a monstrous growth and strength of body."

The doom of the world was immediately pronounced after the commission of the antediluvian sin. Prophecy intimates, according to the twelfth and thirteenth chapters of Revelation, that future confinement of angels of darkness to the earth plane will call forth the Lord Jesus Christ in flaming fire to take vengeance.

That Hades will be emptied, in part, during the final climax of horror, is indicated by the words: "And I looked, and behold a pale horse: and his name that sat on him was Death, and Hades followed with him."

The rider of the red and bloodstained horse will have previously mounted his vicious steed and swiftly gone forth with a great sword to take peace from the earth.

The black horse, driven under the lash of famine, will have sped on his errand of destruction.

And now, the twin destroyers, Death and Hades, on the pale horse, compel a guilty world to drink to its dregs the cup of wrath.

Let it be remarked parenthetically that our chief con-
cern is with the red horse, since this beast may be seen
moving over the face of the earth in the crisis now engulfing
the nations. Its course will finally terminate in judgment.

Leaders of the international red conspiracy may seem
to be above restraint for a time. They may conspire to wipe
Christianity from the face of the earth and make atheism
the religion of all mankind. They may think to protect themselves behind the folds of an iron curtain. But they will
eventually encounter the stern wrath of an outraged God.
"Vengeance is mine; I will repay, saith the Lord."

★   ★   ★

A LTHOUGH THIS TREATISE is concerned primarily with
the symbolic meaning of the four horses of the Apocalypse, to pause here without introducing the fifth into the
discussion would be the equivalent to an anti-climax.

"And I saw heaven opened, and behold a white horse;
and he that sat upon him was called Faithful and True,
and in righteousness he doth judge and make war. His eyes
were as a flame of fire, and on his head were many crowns;
and he had a name written, that no man knew, but he himself. And he was clothed in a vesture dipped in blood: and
his name is called The Word of God." Revelation 19:11-13.

CHAPTER TWO

Communism In Ezekiel

THE COMMUNIST MOVEMENT of the twentieth century stems from Satanic forces that have operated from the remote past. It existed, back in Old Testament times, as a conspiracy against the plan and purpose of God.

The prophet Ezekiel devoted the thirty-eighth chapter of his book to predicting its appearance in modern form. The first six verses of the document demand special attention at this time.

Verse 1. And the word of the Lord came unto me, saying,

Verse 2. Son of man, set thy face against Gog, the land of Magog, the chief prince of Meshech and Tubal, and prophesy against him,

Verse 3. And say, Thus saith the Lord God; Behold I am against thee, O Gog, the chief prince of Meshech and Tubal:

Verse 4. And I will turn thee back, and put hooks into thy jaws, and I will bring thee forth, and all thine army, horses and horsemen, all of them clothed with all sorts of armour, even a great company with bucklers and shields, all of them handling swords:

Verse 5.   Persia, Ethiopia, and Libya with them; all of them with shield and helmet:

Verse 6. Gomer, and all his bands; the house of Togarmah of the north quarters, and all his bands: and many people with thee.

A word study will serve to illuminate this passage. The prophecy indicates that a powerful nation described as Gog, situated in the north, will unite with other peoples and form a gigantic military combination. The eighth verse announces that this will occur in "the latter years."

Old Testament Reds

THE SCOFIELD BIBLE footnote at the bottom of this chapter reads as follows: "That the primary reference is to the northern European powers, headed by Russia, all agree. 'Gog' is the prince; 'Magog' is his land. The reference to Meshech and Tubal, Moscow and Tobolsk, is a clear mark of identification."

An analysis of the context shows that the term Gog is associated with the color of red. It is significant that Communists of our day are called "reds."

By way of background it should be noted that Esau was the first red. Concerning his birth Genesis 25:24-25 says: "And when her days to be delivered were fulfilled, behold, there were twins in her womb. And the first came out red, all over like a hairy garment; and they called his name Esau."

In later years, when his birthright was being sold to Jacob, he specified that the pottage had to be red. "Feed me, I pray thee, with that same red pottage." Thereupon the name Esau was changed to Edom, which means red.

Esau's descendents were called Edomites—or redites. They were the reds of Old Testament times. Because Amalek was a grandson of Esau, the family line became known as Amalekites. The number multiplied into a large clan and their record for mischief and viciousness is unsurpassed in Bible history. Moses said: "The Lord will have war with Amalek from generation to generation."

Beginning about one thousand years before Christ the term Agag became the permanent title for a succession of Amalekitish rulers. The appellation was used to denote an office, the occupant of which was literally "king of the reds."

The criminal record of one particular member of the dynasty is given in the fifteenth chapter of First Samuel. His execution was finally ordered by divine decree. The term Gog is derived from Agag. It means defiance of God. The definition suggests the upraised arm and clenched fist shaken against God in heaven. The term Agag symbolized the reds of ancient times. The term Gog symbolizes the reds of modern times.

Ezekiel's inspired prophecy is addressed to the times in which we live. It is significant that God should have prompted him to say: "I am against thee, O Gog." The inference is clear. Atheism is the religion of international Communism. The reds of the twentieth century are against God, and He is therefore against them.

The word "chief" of Ezekiel 38:2 is a proper noun, Rosh, in the original, rather than an adjective. "I am against thee, O Gog, Rosh prince," would be a correct rendering. The name Russia is derived from Rosh.

Meshech is the root word for Moscow. Lenin and Trotsky found the capital of Russia in St. Petersburg. They contributed to the fulfillment of Ezekiel's prophecy by transferring the seat of government to Moscow. The Soviets boast of taking the Bible out of Russia ... but they have not taken themselves out of the Bible!

Russia's Origin

DR. CHARLES MARSTON, an authority on archaeological subjects, comments on this portion of Scripture as follows:

"These are the progenitors as proved not only from locality but from descent of the Russians; the name Russian being derived from Rosh; Muscovy or Muscovites being derived from Meshech; and Tubal being the origin of Tobolsk. You may, in short trace by names that exist in Russia, as well as by national and geographical distribution of races, to the ancient arrangement specified clearly and distinctly in Genesis 10, and referred to by Ezekiel.

"Now these names and this identification I have already

said are not formed to suit Scriptures to present events. Bishop Lowth, than whom there was no more sober interpreter of prophecy, says: 'Rosh, taken as a proper name in Ezekiel signifies the inhabitants of Scythia, from whom the modern Russians derive their name.' This is the judgment of a very wise and learned Bishop.

"Thus taking the maps I have mentioned where the ancient dispersion is arranged; taking the lineal, genealogical descent of these heads or fathers of the nations, we arrive at the conclusion that Rosh, Meschech and Tubal find their descendents at this moment in the Northern and Southern parts of Russia, by the Euxine Sea, the Sea of Azoff, the Don, the Dnieper, and among the Cossacks."

A study of ancient maps, in comparison with the description of races given in Genesis 10 and Ezekiel 38, will add to the fund of information now extant. Special attention is due the British Benziger Bible, an old book printed in England, bearing a Preface by the Cardinal Archbishop of Westminister. Its early pages contain this note: "Translated from the Latin Vulgate and diligently compared with other editions in divers languages."

This Bible has several very old maps which contain the Scriptural names now under consideration and locates them in their proper geographical positions.

The word Magog appears in the region north of the Caspian Sea, which is now southern Russia. The word Gomer is spread across the area where modern Germany is located. The word Meshech is near the shores of the Black Sea. Genesis 10:3 names Ashkenaz as a son of Gomer, and the Benziger maps show the original name of the Black Sea to have been the "Sea of Ashkenaz."

Inspiration and Ethnology

IN THE YEAR 1855, almost one hundred years ago, the Reverend Doctor Cumming, F. R. S. E., delivered a remarkable lecture at Crown Court Chapel of London, England, wherein he traced the lineage of Russia according to the phraseology of Ezekiel. He said:

"My identification of the names in Ezekiel 38, is not the result of trying to accomodate God's Word to present eventualities but of accepting what the most able geographers and ethnologists h a v e independently ascertained before; and showing that they are—viewed scientifically—irrespective altogether of the prediction or of what the prediction applies to; the representatives of well-known nations now existing. The names here given are Gog, Magog, Meshech, Tubal, Persia, Cush, Put, Gomer, Togarmah, Sheba, Dedan and Tarhich.

"If we refer to the tenth chapter of Genesis we shall there find the whole of these tribes mentioned with their dispersion. The sons of Japheth are Gomer and Magog and Madai and Javan and Tubal and Meschech and Tiras. And the sons of Gomer, Ashkenaz and Ripath and Togarmah; and the sons of Javan; Elishah and Tarhish, Kittim and Dodanim.

"If you will look into that valuable edition of the Scriptures—Bagster's Polyglot Bible—you will find in the very first map an account of these peoples covering the different localities over which these very nations are said to have been scattered.

"You will find, for instance, the whole Northern portion

of Europe occupied by Tubal, Meshech and Magog; the arrangements constructed from the sacred record. Tracing the history geographically from this map we find that Magog, one of the descendents mentioned in Genesis 10, is settled on the east and northeast of the Euxine or Black Sea, and part of the Russian Empire, including the rivers Don and Dnieper and the neighbourhood of the Caucasus. These tribes all settled in these very districts.

"Pliny the Roman writer says: 'Hierapolis taken by the Scythians was afterwards called Magog,' one of the names here given. Josephus, the Jewish historian says, 'The Scythians were called by the Greeks, Magog.' The very name Caucasus is derived from two Oriental words—Gog and Chasan—meaning, Gog's fortified place. So that when we read of the 'Caucasus,' we are reading of the mountains of Gog's fortified place or Gog's fort, the very name of these mountains indicating the family or race with which by proximity they were intimately associated.

"When the Danes or Northmen first landed in the neighborhood of Lisbon (A. D. 843) they were called by the Arabians, Magioges, i. e., 'the people of Gog and Magog.'

"Meshech, another of these Scripture names, is found under the name of Moschi or the Maesi inhabiting the Moschic mountains, east of the Black Sea. Josephus says that the Moscheni were founded by Meshech, and the Thobelites by Tubal. As if to show the identity, Tubal means in Arabic—iron.

"The Greeks, also deriving a name from the same source,

called the same people—Chalybs—the Greek word, which also means iron or steel. Now, these two races, the descendents of Meshech and the descendents of Magog, are all found at this time in the southern part of the Russian Empire in the provinces of Georgia, and Cacasus and the Sea of Azoff, and on the Don and on the Dneiper.

"Their descendents penetrated into the deserts of Scythia, and peopled subsequent to their first introduction, the northern parts of Russia. The Sarmatians or the Muscovites came from Pontus in Asia Minor, the very province in which they first settled, and to which we traced the descendents of Meshech and Tubal. The rover, Araxes, was called in Arabic, Rosh, and the people dwelling upon its banks were called by the Oriental, 'Rosh'."

★   ★   ★

BRIMSTONE is associated with atomic energy both in Scripture and modern science. Ezekiel 38:22 describes Russia's climactic judgment and leaves no doubt that it will be visited with a rain of atomic fire. "And I will plead against him (Gog) with pestilence and with blood; and I will rain upon him, and upon his bands, and upon the many people that are with him, an overflowing rain, and great hailstones, fire, and brimstone."

In that day, the red horse of the Apocalypse will be brought under control, hence the prophecy of Ezekiel 38:4, "I will turn thee back, and put hooks into thy jaws."

CHAPTER THREE

Communism In History

DISORDERS, revolutions, mob violence and economic convulsions do not happen. They result from planning. Plots, schemes, tricks and intrigues are fomented behind the scenes and hatched beneath the surface.

Subterranean fires thus lighted eventually reach the surface in a conflagration. The rank and file of people are taken off guard. There comes a devastating outburst. Lives are lost, property destroyed, and the progress of liberty interrupted.

Then the sleeping masses awaken, yawn, stir themselves and deplore the wreckage. Designing leaders fasten shackles upon the nation and tedious steps toward human liberty have to start all over again.

International conspirators frequently lull masses of people to sleep until their plots are so far advanced that nothing can stop them. A man in a stupor is helpless. Despoilers have ways for keeping the public mind befuddled, drugged, and under the influence of opiates. Disraeli once said: "The world is governed by very different personages from what is imagined by those who are not behind the scenes."

Propaganda is a powerful weapon in the hands of vicious

men. The thinking of a whole nation may be warped in a comparatively short time by a bombardment of ideas from carefully planned and timed sources. By degrees these ideas sink into the mass mind and the community is moulded accordingly. Cross currents are created and hatreds generated. True purposes are concealed. Professional destroyers frequently say one thing publicly while privately shaping their policies along exactly the opposite lines.

A populace thus deceived, takes for granted the things taught them and thereafter perform like croaking frogs of the Apocalypse. They come under the influence of a "strong delusion, that they should believe a lie; that they might all be damned."

The average person lives on the surface and neither cares, nor knows how to inform himself about secret conspiracies operating for his destruction. He prefers to "eat, drink and be merry" and resents being brought face to face with the unpleasant truth. The American people are too gullible.

Fraternal societies founded to enunciate high ideals are sometimes perverted by men of evil genius who gain control. Secret orders have at various times in history provided convenient cloaks for subversionists to use in spreading revolutionary doctrines. It will be shown in this treatise that the Communist conspiracy came into existence under such circumstances.

Two revolutions of comparatively recent times, connected by an underground organization, owe their success to the foregoing line of attack—the French revolution and the Russian revolution.

Neither of these outbreaks resulted from legitimate causes to relieve the suffering of poor and middle class people. Such public affirmations by the leaders were only pretexts. The chains of slavery imposed upon the duped followers of the Robespierres, Lenins, Trotskys, Stalins and Molotovs prove that the conspirators did not have the welfare of the masses at heart.

Both of these holocausts resulted from secret planning so that an invisible empire could enslave a large section of the human race. The motivation was anti-christ and Satanic, with the Christian religion becoming the chief target of opposition.

Disraeli delivered a significant address before the English House of Commons on July 14, 1856 in which he said:

"It is useless to deny, because it is impossible to conceal, that a great part of Europe—the whole of Italy and France and a great portion of Germany, to say nothing of other countries—is covered with a network of these secret societies, just as the superficies of the earth is now being covered with railroads. And what are their objects? They do not attempt to conceal them. They do not want constitutional government; they do not want ameliorated institutions. They want to change the tenure of land, to drive out the present owners of the soil and to put an end to ecclesiastical establishments."

Darkness and Light

THE COMMUNIST MOVEMENT can be traced in a direct line as an organized conspiracy back to the middle

of the eighteenth century. Beyond that date it becomes some-
what nebulous as far as written records   are   concerned.
The history of the movement   is geared   to the story of
Illuminism.

Bible-believing Christians detect in this weird system
of occultism a demonic principle, capable of warping the
minds of men, by powers that transcend human levels.   It
existed in Apostolic times and is described   in the   New
Testament as the "mystery of iniquity."

The Satanic source of Illuminism   is   exposed in the
Apostle Paul's letter to the Ephesians: "For we wrestle
not against flesh and blood,   but against principalities,
against powers, against the rulers of the darkness of this
world, against spiritual wickedness in high places."

As divine illumination is experienced in the soul of
the believer through contact with the Holy Spirit, so also
there is a counterfeit light that poisons   human thought
and produces decay. There are "seducing spirits" that im-
pregnate human minds with "doctrines of devils."

There is a white light of spiritual illumination.   But
there is also a black light of demonic illumination. "Satan
himself is transformed into an angel of light." Illuminism is black magic. Jannes and Jambres manipulated these
powers in the days of Moses. The attack is as old as sin
on this planet.

Hidden intelligences, using humans as pawns, mean
to blot Christ's cause and Christian civilization from the
face of the earth. The Holy Spirit working through good
people operates as a restraining power. "For the mystery

of iniquity doth already work: only he who now hindereth will hinder, until he be taken out of the way. And then
shall that wicked be revealed."

Satan is the mastermind behind Illuminism. Jesus said:
"I beheld Satan as lightning fall from heaven." Satanic
light fills the earth. This accounts for the fact that the
world is in darkness.

Christians are like bright lights shining in a dark place.
"But if we walk in the light, as he is in the light, we have
fellowship one with another, and the blood of Jesus Christ
his Son cleanseth us from all sin." "For ye were sometimes
darkness, but now are ye light in the Lord: walk as children of light."

The Encyclopaedia Britannica says that the term Illuminism has been for centuries used by mystic groups to
indicate the reception of "light" being "directly com-
municated to them from a higher source, or as due to a
clarified and exalted condition of the human intelligence."

The same authority finds Illuminism emerging from
among the Gnostics at the beginning of the Christian era.
Gnosticism polluted several worship centers of the early
Church. It promoted spiritism and immoral sexual practices
and taught that reason surpassed faith.

Even sacred communion services were turned into
orgies of eating, drinking and dissipation. Paul found it
necessary to purge the Church at Corinth of these practices.
This is indicated by the following rebuke in his first Cor-
inthian letter: "Ye cannot drink the cup of the Lord, and

the cup of devils: ye cannot be partakers of the Lord's table, and of the table of devils."

One of the earliest and most prominent Gnostic leaders was a man of Jewish nationality named Simon Magus. Bishop George Lavington of the Anglican Church says:

"These were Heretics, and, that they were Heretics of the worst kind that ever defiled and disgraced the Christian Name, is allowed by all Denominations of Christians.

"Some of these lived in the first century and even in the Apostles' Day, but the second century was most fruitful in the Production of this Generation of Vipers and we must receive our Knowledge of their abominable Tenets from the early Ecclesiastical Writers such as Irenaeus, Epiphanius, Theodoret and many others . . .

"Such was the Excellency of their Knowledge and Illumination, who arrogantly styled themselves Gnostics, that they are superior to Peter or Paul or any of Christ's other disciples. They only, have drunk up the supreme Knowledge, are above Principalities and Powers, secure of Salvation: and for that very reason are free to debauch Women, or indulge all manner of Licentiousness.

"Simon Magus, who taught that his Harlot Helena was the Holy Ghost, instituted certain foul and infamous Mysteries inexpressibly filthy and had Assemblies equally filthy to celebrate them: These being the Mysteries of Life, and of the most perfect Knowledge.

"For this end they taught Incontinence to be obligatory, as a Law; and not only lawful, but necessary to

Salvation; not only compatible with the Saviour's Religion, but an essential Part of it: and those were the best Men, who in the common Opinion were the most vicious.

"For which Reason, in their Feasts, the Candles were extinguished, each lay with the Women, as Chance appointed; and they called this Lasciviousness a mystical Initiation, a mystical Communion . . . What was abominable in others, being highly meritorious in themselves."

Thus Bishop Lavington traced the early gleams of Illuminism to their source. He isolated the first germs of a system that was destined to bring pain and misery to the entire human family.

Historians have followed the trail of Illuminism down across the centuries, noting its manifestations in various ways at different times, to the present hour.

The Trail of the Serpent

THE BEGINNING of the fourteenth century witnessed the appearance of an occult society known as the Brotherhood of the Rose Croix, which professed a secret existence dating into the distant past. The leaders of the organization were alchemists, astrologers and spiritists. They professed to be seeking a process to transmute base metals into gold and an explanation for the secret of life.

The order came boldly into the open in 1614 by issuing two books, "Fama Fraternitatis" and the "Confessio," from the pen of their principal leader, Valentin Andrea. He was appointed chaplain to the Duke of Brunswick Wolfenbuttel twenty‑

six years later. The entrance of this man and his teachings into the Brunswick family becomes significant, when one considers the important part played by a descendant, the Duke of Brunswick, in the French Revolution.

Valentin Andrea was born in 1586 and died at the age of sixty-eight. His writings dealt with the legendary existence and travels of a mythical figure called Christian Rosenkreutz. A study of the fable, written for the purpose of conveying a secret message to adherents, shows that the cult provides an important link in the chain of Illuminism.

Christian Rosenkreutz was allegedly born in Germany in the year 1378. As a young man he made a pilgrimage to the Holy Land. He later met "Wise Men of Arabia" who contributed to his schooling in mystic lore. Then he visited Egypt and made advanced studies in the mystries of life, nature and the universe. He mastered the Jewish Cabala.

Being destined to live one hundred and six years, he died back home in 1484. After bringing the wisdom of the ages together and compounding it into one philosophy, he gave the secret to three disciples and spent the closing days of life in solitude. His disciples enshrouded him and disappeared.

His burial place was prophesied to remain a mystery for six times twenty years. At the end of this period it was to become a hearth, from which a great light would go forth to Illuminate the world.

In the year 1604 a group of Illuminated ones were guided

to his grave. On entering the cave they found it to be resplendent with a bright light. It contained an altar with a copper plate bearing the inscription, "Living, I reserved this light for my grave." There were lamps burning in the sacred precincts without fuel.

Mrs. Nesta Webster says: "I suggest that Christian Rosenkreutz was a purely mythical personage, and that the whole legend concerning his travels was invented to disguise the real sources whence the Rosicrucians derived their system, which would appear to have been a compound of ancient esoteric doctrines, of Arabian and Syrian magic, and of Jewish Cabalism. Rosicrucianism thus became in the seventeenth century a generic title by which everything of the nature of Cabalism, Theosophy, Alchemy, Astrology, and Mysticism was designated."

The third edition of Encyclopaedia Britannica, published in 1797, contains an article about the Brotherhood of the Rose Croix in which we read: " A name assumed by a sect or cabal of hermetical philosophers; who arose, as it has been said, or at least became first taken notice of in Germany, in the beginning of the fourteenth century. They bound themselves together by a solemn secret. . .

"Because they pretended to protect the period of human life, by means of certain nostrums, and even to restore youth, they were called Immortals; as they pretended to know all things, they have been called Illuminati; and because they have made no appearance for several years, unless the sect of Illuminated which lately started up on the continent (of Europe) derives its origin from them, they have been called the Invisible Brothers."

Lady Queensborough says: "Subsequent research upon the organization of the Fraternity, its tenets and its achievements, shows it to have been a medium for the propagation of Gnosticism and a centre for political activities."

Among the leaders of the order who became prominent during the era when seeds of destruction aimed at Christianity and orderly government were being sown in Europe, was one Faustus Socinius.

This man, born in 1539, commanded a large following. His avowed hatred for the Church caused both Protestants and Catholics to oppose him. Operating like a twentieth century Communist, he tried by stealth and intrigue to instill a negative philosophy into the existing religious organizations. He engaged himself in founding an association, the aims of which were to be subversive to everything for which the Church stood.

Socinius encountered opposition and was forced to spend the last two years of his life in seclusion. He died in the year 1604. Thirteen years later, the Brotherhood reaffirmed its devotion to his teachings and "renewed its oath to destroy the Church of Jesus Christ."

Centuries were required for the forces of Illuminism, motivated by Satan, to generate the subterranean flame that would eventually produce a world-wide holocaust. Andrea, Socinius and others of the middle ages were harbingers to Weishaupt, Marx, Lenin, Trotsky, Molotov, Stalin, Laski, Browder, Roosevelt and Foster.

Other Manifestations of Illuminism

PROMOTERS OF ILLUMINISM in Spain founded an organization called the Alombrados about the year 1520. Ignatius Loyola, while a student at Salamanca, was tried in 1527 by an ecclesiastical commission on the charge of sympathizing with the cult. He was acquitted and later founded the Jesuit order.

During the middle of the eighteenth century, Illuminism came to public notice in Sweden, through the establishment of an order known as the Illuminati of Stockholm.

The Illuminati of Avignon was the name chosen by a group of French destructionists in 1760. Antoine Pernety, an unfrocked Benedictine monk and Cabalist, was the leader. He later founded a similar organization in Paris known as Theosophical Illumines.

Wherever the doctrine of Illuminism came into prominence, its exponents were found professing superior knowledge over the secrets of nature. They were portrayed as possessing mysterious medicines, strange poisons, weird nostrums, and an esoteric knowledge of religion and philosophy.

In the fourteenth century, the term Rosicrucianism became a cover name for a conglomeration of occult ideas promulgated by Gnostics, Illuminates and their ilk in the fourteenth and fifteenth centuries. The system at that time encompassed an accumulation of subversive elements from the dawn of the Christian era.

The foregoing record of Illuminism is sufficiently complete to show its evil character. It existed for centuries as an unorganized system of black magic counterfeiting Gospel truth. Finally there appeared on the scenes a man by the name of Adam Weishaupt with sufficient capacity to co-ordinate the many branches and reduce it to a philosophy. On May 1, 1776 he founded "The Illuminati."

★   ★   ★

SUFFICIENT has been written to expose the Satanic background from which the present anti-christ conspiracy emerged. The program is now coming to fruition on a worldwide scale. A conflict is raging between the forces of Christ and· Antichrist.

Leaders of modern Communism, descendants of Illuminism, have cause to fear the New Testament Gospel. When faithfully proclaimed, it creates a climate in which the forces of anti-christ become paralyzed. This explains why Lunacharsky, previously quoted, also said: "We hate Christianity and the Christians. Even the best of them must be regarded as our worst eenmies. They teach love. What we want is hatred."

The Holy Spirit is in the world as a restraining agency against all forms of evil. To the degree that He finds human avenues through whom to work, anti-christ is negated. The Apostle Paul referred to Illuminism in his day as "the mystery of iniquity" and exalted the third person of the eternal Trinity as a deterrent in the same verse of Scripture: "For the mystery of iniquity doth already work: only he (the Holy Spirit) who now hindereth will hinder, until he be taken out of the way." II Thessalonians 2:7.

CHAPTER FOUR

Adam Weishaupt, Human Devil

L OUIS BLANC, the French writer, described Dr. Adam Weishaupt as "one of the deepest conspirators that ever existed."

This mysterious man who so cleverly concealed his identity as to be scarcely known beyond research circles was born in southern Germany, February 6, 1748. As a young man he occupied the chair of Canon Law in Ingolstadt University. Although hidden from view, he was the most powerful figure of his day. He set in motion forces that destroyed millions of lives and left his mark of evil upon all future generations.

Weishaupt used men to carry forward his plots like a carpenter uses tools. It is remarkable how his followers succeeded in keeping him out of sight. His vanity did not require public acclaim. He was content to plant seeds of destruction and wait patiently for them to germinate. There is no variation from the rule that the real authors of confusion never show themselves.

In his book "Lexicon of Freemasonry," Gallatin Mackey, close friend and confidant of Albert Pike, said: "Weishaupt was a radical in politics and an infidel in religion, and he organized this association, not more for the purpose of aggrandizing himself, than of overturning Christianity and the institutions of society."

On one occasion Weishaupt wrote to an intimate friend: "My circumstances necessitate that I should remain hidden from most of the members as long as I live. I am obliged to do everything through five or six persons." On another occasion he said: "One must show how easy it would be for one clever head to direct hundreds of thousands of men."

Again he wrote: "I have two immediately below me

DR. ADAM WEISHAUPT

into whom I breathe my whole spirit, and each of these two has again two others, and so on. In this way I can set a thousand men in motion and on fire in the simplest manner, and in this way one must impart orders and operate on politics."

Weishaupt understood the evil powers he was releasing. He was conscious of the magnitude of his crime. On one occasion he explained: "What it costs me to read, study, think, write, cross out, and rewrite!"

The demonic intelligence operating through his personality made heavy demands upon soul and body. The thought uppermost in his mind was to devise schemes and intrigues for destroying the existing order. He was shrewd enough to see what might be accomplished if the lodge rooms of Europe could be brought under his control.

A Cloak for Crime

SHORTLY BEFORE the French Revolution we find the Marquis de Luchet saying: "This society aims at governing the world. Its object is universal domination." He called the Illuminati, "A subterranean fire smouldering eternally and breaking forth periodically in violent and devastating explosions." He pleaded with Masons to open their eyes and save their Order from these corrupting influences. "Would it not be possible to direct the Freemasons themselves against the Illumines by showing them that whilst they are working to maintain harmony in society, those others everywhere are sowing seeds of discord?"

FREEMASONRY IN AMERICA, AND FREEMASON-

RY IN EUROPE ARE AS DIFFERENT AS DAY FROM NIGHT. This fact should be borne in mind as one examines Weishaupt's successes in perverting the order on the continent of Europe. The Illuminati changed its lodge rooms into underground breeding places of crime, anarchy, atheism and violence.

Abbe Barruel, a French patriot and Catholic priest who lived contemporaneously with Weishaupt, wrote voluminously about the relation of the illumined lodges to the French Revolution. Barruel also made an examination into the life and personal traits of the subject of our discussion. "The man who invented his Illuminism only to convert it into the common sewer of every anti-Christian and anti-social error," is the way he speaks of Weishaupt.

In his book "Anti-Christian Conspiracy," Barruel tells about a young man who started out to become an Illuminatus but reversed his attitude. The report shows how Weishaupt and his "adepts" began by giving the prospective initiate small doses of poison to be increased as it took effect.

Barruel says: " I shall mention Toussaint, as this man shows to what height atheism raged among the conspirators. He had undertaken the part of the corruption of morals. Under the mask of moderation, he succeeds by telling youth that nothing was to be feared from love, this passion only perfecting them. That between man and woman that was a sufficient claim on each other without matrimony. That children are not more beholden to their fathers for their birth than for the champagne they had drunk or the minuet they had been pleased to dance. That the wicked had nothing to fear from the punishments of another world.

Nothwithstanding all this doctrine the conspirators looked on him as a timid adept because he owned a God in heaven, and a soul in man; and to punish him they styled him the Capuchin Philosopher. Happily for him he took a better way of punishing them by abandoning their cause and recanting from his errors."

To Barruel we are indebted in part for information about a Jew by the name of Kolmer, who collaborated with Weishaupt in creating the mysteries and degrees of his so-called higher Masonry. Kolmer, a genius in black art, was a Cabalist from Egypt.

Five years intervened between the time Kolmer first called on Weishaupt and the day when it was officially announced that members could be accepted into the order. These years were devoted to perfecting plans for an assault upon Christianity and the governments of the world.

At last Weishaupt was ready to say: "We shall have a Masonic lodge of our own. We shall regard this as our nursery garden. To some Masons we shall not at once reveal that we have something more than the Masons have. At every opportunity we shall cover ourselves with this (Masonry). All those who are not suited to the work shall remain in the Masonic Lodge and advance in without knowing anything of the further system."

Thus he introduced an alleged super-Masonry with himself as the dominant power. He led Masons to believe there was a higher, much older and more mysterious system than they understood or possessed. Before a great while

he was able to place key men into strategic positions bringing the Order under his personal control.

He was animated with one desire, namely to destroy,
destroy, destroy. He ruled Masonry with one thought in
mind—to use it as an instrument of destruction for ex-
terminating Christianity and leveling governments to the
ground.

Robison's Famous Report

WHEN THE BAVARIAN GOVERNMENT finally fer-
reted out the conspiracy and arrested the leaders, it
was discovered that they possessed weird poisons and had
no compunctions about employing   them   to silence opposition.

Leaders used a powder which produced   blindness.
They had a formula that   "devoured everything" when
sprayed in the face. They also possessed a strange sub-
stance called Luisenwasser (Louise Water) because it was
secretly given to Louise, the Crown Princess of Saxony to
further the romance with Toselli and thereby detract from
the reputation of the ruling dynasty.   These   and other
secrets were made known to the government when it con-
fiscated the lodge property of the organization on August
16, 1785.

Weishaupt was trained as a Jesuit. He later renounced
the order. But the schooling received and insight gained
into its secrets and methods of operation stood him well in
building an occult system peculiarly his own.

In the prologue to her book, "The French Revolution," Mrs. Nesta Webster says: "Weishaupt, who had been educated by the Jesuits, succeeded in persuading two other ex-Jesuits to join him in organizing the new Order, and it was no doubt this circumstance that gave rise to the belief entertained by certain contemporaries that the Jesuits were the secret directors of the sect. The truth is more probably that Illuminism was founded on the regime of the Jesuits although their religious doctrines were diametrically opposed."

While Barruel was assembling his material about the plot in France, another scholar by the name of Professor John Robison, a Scotch Protestant, was carrying on a similar investigation in the British Isles. Robison was a loyal Mason who loved his lodge fervently. After making a tour of the lodges of continental Europe, he returned to the British Isles and published his findings in a treatise entitled, "Proofs of a Conspiracy against all the Religions and Governments of Europe, carried on by secret meetings of Free Masons, Illuminati and Reading Societies, collected from good authorities by the Author, Professor of Natural Philosophy and Secretary of the Royal Society of Edinburgh."

Robison published his work in the year 1798 and died shortly thereafter under mysterious circumstances. He said that both in France and Germany, "The lodges had become the haunts of many projectors and fanatics, both in science, in religion, and in politics, who had availed themselves of the secrecy and freedom of speech maintained in these meetings. In their hands Freemasonry became a thing totally unlike, and almost in direct opposition to, the system imported from England, where the rule was observed that nothing touching religion or government shall ever be spoken of in the lodges," and finally fell under the influence of an association whose leaders "disbelieved every word that they uttered and every doctrine that they taught," and whose "real intention was to abolish all religion, overturn every government and make the world a general plunder and wreck."

The noted Scotch Protestant further stated that the Order of the Illuminati "abjured Christianity, advocated sensual pleasures, believed in annihilation, and called patriotism and loyalty narrow-minded prejudices incompatible with universal benevolence;" further, "they accounted all princes usurpers and tyrants, and all privileged orders as their abettors; they meant to abolish the laws which protected property accumulated by long continued and successful industry; and to prevent for the future any such accumulation, they intended to establish universal liberty and equality, the imprescriptible rights of man, and as preparation for all this they intended to root out all religion and ordinary morality, and even to break the bonds of domestic life, by destroying the veneration for marriage-vows, and by taking the education of children out of the hands of the parents."

Weishaupt's Program in America

THESE SAME negative, destructionist doctrines form the basis of the international Communist movement of the twentieth century. Robison's explanation of how Weishaupt's disciples disseminated their teachings and poisoned the thinking of unsuspecting multitudes, shows that the order used the identical methods employed by Communists and fellow-travelers today.

After examining the writings of Barruel, Robison wrote: "This author (Barruel) confirms all that I have said of the Enlighteners, whom he very aptly calls Philosophists; and of the abuses of Freemasonry in France. He shows, unquestionably, that a formal and systematic conspiracy against Religion was formed and zealously prosecuted by Voltaire, d'Alembert and Diderot, assisted by Frederick II, King of Prussia; and I see that their principles and their manner of procedure have been the same with those of the German atheists and anarchists.

"Like them they hired an army of writers; they industriously pushed their writings into every house and every cottage. Those writings were equally calculated for inflaming the sensual appetites of men and for perverting their judgements. They endeavored to get the command of the schools, particularly those for the lower classes; and they erected and managed a prodigious number of Circulating Libraries and Reading Societies. They took the name of Economists and affected to be continually occupied with plans for improving Commerce, Manufactures, Agriculture, Finance, etc., and published from time to time respectable performances on those subjects.

"But their darling project was to destroy Christianity and all religion, and to bring about a total change of government. They employed writers to compose corrupting and impious books—these were revised by the Society and corrected until they suited their purpose. A number were printed in a handsome manner, to defray the expense; and then a greater number were printed in the cheapest form possible and given for nothing, or at very low prices to hawkers and peddlers with the injunction to distribute them secretly through the cities and villages."

If Professor Robison were living today he could not describe more accurately the tricks and schemes employed before our eyes, in accomplishing the same objectives for which the Illuminati was created.

While the Illuminati possessed an esoteric and mystical side, this was not the phase in which Weishaupt was most deeply concerned. Mrs. Webster remarks significantly: "On the contrary, the more we penetrate into his system, the more apparent it becomes that all the formulas he employs which derive from any religious source—whether Persian, Egyptian, or Christian—merely serve to distinguish a purely material purpose, a plan for destroying the existing order of society."

Weishaupt prostituted continental Masonry because it was the most practical tool available for accomplishment of the purposes he had in mind. Men who came under the hypnotic spell of his new degrees found themselves confused and incapable of longer living normal law-abiding lives. Local lodges thus perverted, became spawns of vice and revolution. It was in these underground centers that the crimes of the French Revolution were hatched.

An Illuminized lodge was one that yielded to the destructive principles of Weishaupt and the technique of promoting revolution. By this means he was able to bore beneath the surface and undermine every government in Europe.

Robinson's analysis shows that the Illuminati program included the six following propositions:

1. Abolition of all ordered government.
2. Abolition of inheritance.
3. Abolition of private property.
4. Abolition of patriotism.
5. Abolition of family.
6. Abolition of religion.

These are the six basic principles of Communism as we know it today. All of these have been applied in Russia and other countries that have come under the curse of the hammer and sickle. The modern "Weishaupts" of Moscow expect to carry his dream to completion and wreck the world. A little thinking will therefore show that Communisim is not new. These studies trace the conspiracy back to May 1, 1776, the day the Illuminati came officially into existence.

Illuminated Jacobin Clubs

WEISHAUPT'S METHOD for boring into existing organizations, paralleling the schemes used by the Communist propagandists of our time, is illustrated in the following letter which he wrote to a fellow Illuminatus: "We must consider how we can begin to work under another form. If only the aim is achieved, it does not matter under what cover it takes place, and a cover is always necessary. For in concealment lies a great part of our strength. For this reason we must cover ourselves with the name of another society. The lodges that are under

Freemasonry are in the meantime the most suitable cloak for our high purpose, because the world is already accustomed to expect nothing great from them which merits attention. As in the spiritual Orders of the Roman Church, religion was, alas! only a pretense, so must our Order also in a nobler way try to conceal itself behind a learned society or something of the kind. A society concealed in this manner cannot be worked against. We shall be shrouded in impenetrable darkness from spies and emissaries of other societies."

Students of history will recall that political clubs known as the Jacobins held the balance of power in the French Revolution. Among the early members of these organizations were Mirabeau and Robespierre. The Encyclopaedia Britannica says: "By August 10, 1790, there were already one hundred and fifty-two affiliated clubs, and at the close of 1791 the Jacobins had a network of branches all over France. It was this widespread yet highly centralized organization that gave to the Jacobin Club its formidable power. The secret of their strength was this: in the midst of general disorganization, they alone were organized."

From the time the first Jacobin Club was established, these centers were duly Illuminated by Weishaupt's helpers, including such leaders of the sect as Bode and Baron de Busche. The purpose of the Jacobins was "to further the triumph of dogmatic Atheism and create a great social upheaval," explains the French writer Le Forestier. "The members charged with spreading the propaganda of the subversive principles of the club numbered fifty thousand. In 1790, it had twenty thousand livres at its disposal, but at the end of 1791, these had increased to thirty millions."

The history of the Terror of the French Revolution is the history of the Jacobins. And the history of the Jacobins is the history of the Illuminati. Let it be remembered that one of Weishaupt's affectionate titles was "Patriarch of the Jacobins."

Robison exposed the fact, and proved beyond question, that all the leaders of the French Revolution were Illuminati members. One had to be admitted to membership in these ranks to qualify as an instigator of the Terror. "The purpose of initiating members and forming political committees," says Robison, "was to c a r r y through the great plan of a general overturning of religion and government . . . and these committees produced the Jacobin Club."

Mrs. Webster says: "By September, 1791, it was no longer the Legislative Assembly that governed France but the Jacobin Club, of which Robespierre was a leading member." This date, she continues, "found Jacobin Clubs in the towns and villages all over France." and thus the nation was completely undermined and reduced to shambles. "By this means, at a signal from headquarters, insurrection could be organized. Nothing in the history of the French Revolution is more surprising than the skill with which this system was carried out."

A subterranean fire was kindled beneath the institutions of France through the establishment of Illuminated lodge rooms. It came to the surface in the French holocaust. Even a casual examination of the forces that precipitated this orgy of bloodshed, will show an unmistakable similarity with the agencies of Communism which are now trying to gain the ascendancy in our own United States.

Weishaupt, Karl Marx and Stalin

"THE PLAN OF WORLD REVOLUTION devised by Weishaupt has at last been realized," says Mrs. Webster. "We have only to study the course of the revolutionary movement in Europe during the last 130 years to realize that it has been the direct continuation of the scheme of the Illuminati, that the doctrines and the aims of the sect have been handed down without a break through the succeeding groups of revolutionary Socialists.

"All the diabolical methods employed by the Jacobins of France, indoctrinated by the Illuminati, have been repeated in Russia with terrible effect. The danger that threatens civilization is therefore no new danger but dates from before the French Revolution. The blaze kindled by Weishaupt has never ceased to smoulder. France was only the place of its first conflagration."

Karl Marx, to whom modern Communists pay homage, edited his teachings from the doctrines of Weishaupt. The first Communist Manifesto, the bible of the international red movement, published in 1848, is simply a restatement of the Illuminati code.

Points of similarity show the Illuminati, the French Revolution and the Russian Revolution as being inseparably related.

(1) Weishaupt required the leaders of his order to change their names. He took the title of Spartacus. Soon after the turn of the present century, the reds of Germany called themselves Spartacusts instead of Communists.

The leaders of the Russian Revolution likewise changed their names. Zederbaum became Lenin. Bronstein became Trotsky. Finkelstein became Litvinoff. Sobelsohn became Radek. Stalin, Molotov and practically all Communist leaders use aliases like other common criminals. When a person joins the party, he is immediately assigned a fictitious name, given a number and his membership card made out accordingly.

(2) Weishaupt hated Christianity and boasted he was setting in motion forces that would some day destroy the Church of Jesus Christ. Anacharsis Clootz, who stood next to Robespierre in the Legislative Assembly, directed the crusade against Christianity during the French Revolution. He chose as his official title, "Personal Enemy of Jesus Christ." A harlot was exalted as a symbol of worship in Notre Dame cathedral.

"Religion," he wrote, "is a social disease which cannot be too quickly cured. A religious man is a depraved animal; he resembles those beasts that are only kept to be shorn and roasted for the benefit of merchants and butchers. The People is the Sovereign and the God of the world; France is the center of the People-God. Only fools can believe in any God, in a supreme Being."

In like manner, atheism is today the religion of the international Communist movement.

(3) Weishaupt demanded the destruction of all standards of morality. He was himself a pervert. Moral standards were systematically destroyed in the days of the French Revolution. The Communist philosophy, as practiced today, is identical. Children became the property of the state under this system.

(4) Weishaupt advocated abolition of the Christian sabbath. Leaders of the French Revolution destroyed the holy day. Russia has done the same.

(5) Weishaupt founded the Illuminati on May 1, 1776. May day was observed during the French Revolution. Communists all over the world now commemorate the same day.

Turning again to Abbe Barruel's treatise called "Universal Explosion," written in 1797, we find if the word "Bolshevism" were substituted for "Jacobinism," the document would be adapted perfectly to the hour in which we live:

"To whatever government, to whatever religion, to whatever rank of society you belong, if Jacobinism (Bolshevism) wins the day, if the projects and oaths of the sect are accomplished, it is all over with your religion, with your priesthood, with your government and your laws, with your properties and your magistrates. Your riches, your fields, your houses, even to your cottages, all will cease to be yours. You thought the Revolution ended in France, and the Revolution in France was only the first attempt of the Jacobins. In the desires of a terrible and formidable sect you have only reached the first stage of the plans it has formed for that general Revolution which is to overthrow all thrones, all altars, annihilate all property, efface all law, and end by dissolving all society."

CHAPTER FIVE

Communism In America

A N ARMY OF WRITERS trained in the Weishaupt technique of warping minds and poisoning fountains of thought rose in France preceding the French Revolution. Historians agree that without these "scribes of sedition" the blood bath could never have occurred.

Only gullible and uninformed persons doubt that an American Illuminati is now operating in the United States fomenting hatreds toward the Church and orderly government. The methods are similar to those used in France during the latter part of the eighteenth century. The objectives are identical.

This attack upon the America that Christians love is being conducted over the radio, through newspapers, magazines and by word of mouth. News commentators are often carriers of the germ. Study groups and public forums, innocent in appearance, are frequently front organizations for the promotion of subversive doctrines.

Even religious publications are being perverted to serve the same evil purpose. Some ministers of the Gospel have unwittingly become Communists at heart by inbibing poison delivered to them through gaudily printed literature. In her discourse on the undermining of British and American institutions, Mrs. Webster drops this significant remark: "Weishaupt's design of enlisting the clergy in the work of world-revolution has been carried out according to plan."

The 1946 report of the Congressional Committee on Un-American Activities dwells upon the danger of radio being used for the purpose of spreading poison. It shows how men and women, ostensibly broadcasting news from day to day, are engaged in the despicable practice of moulding current thinking to fit the subversive pattern. The Committee examined several of the scripts used by certain so-called commentators, and then stated:

"From the reviews of the scripts of several news commentators it appears that the so-called 'liberal' commentators are all receiving information from the same source, inasmuch, as practically all of them night after night discuss the same subjects and with very little difference in their interpretative language.

"It appears that some commentators are issuing pro-Russian and pro-Communist propaganda. They are endeavoring to secure American support for Russia's foreign policy, some openly and some subtly, and in so doing, they belittle the efforts of the American State Department.

"The commentators have attacked presidential appointees and members of the Congress—particularly those who are opposed to Communism. Certain sections of the American press have been attacked by the commentators and subjected to the name-calling devices of the Communist Party because this section of the press is anti-Russian and anti-communistic.

"The governments of European and Latin American countries have been subjects of attacks by these commentators because they want to see Communism in those countries. These commentators have shown that they would like to see another civil war created in one country of Europe in order to re-establish a communistic regime. Revolutions in several Latin American countries have been advocated by these commentators. In every instance the governments of these countries have been labeled fascist governments.

"General MacArthur and Chiang Kai-shek, who carried the brunt of the sometimes apparently hopeless task of defeating Japan, have been attacked by these commentators. The commentators want MacArthur replaced in Japan because they call his tactics reactionary. Chiang Kai-shek has now become a Fascist to some of these commentators. The commentators have endeavored to create public American sympathy for the Chinese Communists, and have severely criticized Chiang Kai-shek, who is at the head of the recognized Government of China.

"Two of the commentators voicing the party line propaganda have openly advocated the creation of a world state which would embrace Socialism or Communism. They have said this is necessary or else we face destruction. They have urged that we give the atomic secret to Russia as evidence of our good faith. At every turn they want the United States to recognize governments supported by Russia in other countries.

"The American Government has been referred to as the weakest government in the whole world. The same commentator said that the Soviet Russian Government is the most dynamic government on earth."

To correct these abuses, the Committee suggested legislation that would require station owners to (a) make proper and frequent announcements to help the public distinguish between programs consisting of news and those devoted to propaganda; (b) make announcements explaining the name, place of birth, nationality and political affiliation of the commentator, and (c) keep on file for inspection, a set of rules regulating the broadcasting of programs, so that any person aggrieved thereby may apply through the courts for restraints of practices destined to contribute to the weakening of our form of government.

It is safe to say that the majority of American citizens are coming more and more to appreciate the patriotic service rendered by the Committee on Un-American Activities. During the uncertain years of New Dealism this Committee, under the able leadership of such men as Martin Dies, John Rankin, John S. Wood, J. Parnell Thomas and other members of Congress, has survived all attacks and remained inviolate.

Christians and other straight-thinking Americans need to understand that an Illuminati plan, directed by powerful but diseased minds, is functioning in the United States at the present time. The threatened breakdown of our institutions stems from this source. Our plight is the result of planning and conspiring rather than natural disorders.

Blueprint for American Revolution

THE MEN who furnish the driving force for revolutionary movements are able to see far into the future. Some are occultists. Others reason from cause to effect in anticipating trends and changes. They know the necessary wires to pull from behind the scenes. Financial panics, depressions and repressions are sometimes essential creating unrest and unemployment.

The manipulators do not rely upon chance or haphazard methods. They map their attacks like the military strategist.

In the year 1912 a strange book appeared before the public that charted the course of the revolutionary movement in the United States with a degree of accuracy that was almost uncanny. It bore the title, "Philip Dru: Administrator" and was written in parabolic or fictional language.

The writer called it "A Story of Tomorrow." He explained how economic and political crises would produce mob violence, the abolishment of our Constitution, the sacrifice of human liberty and the rise of a totalitarian program. He gave his dictator the name of Philip Dru. That was more than three decades ago, long before Communism, Fascism and Nazism began to replace monarchies and parliamentary systems.

The identity of the author was not disclosed. Many wondered who could write such a cruel, morbid and yet fascinating story. The Jewish publisher would only say that the man who penned the prophecy was prominent in political councils and must necessarily remain anonymous.

The dedication, appearing on the opening page, challenged the American social order with these words: "This book is dedicated to the unhappy many who have lived and died lacking opportunity, because, in the starting, the world-wide social structure was wrongly begun."

This is the premise of the narrative—namely that our form of government is wrong and always has been mortally defective. Communism was offered as something better. But the plight of the enslaved masses, compelled to live under the Moscow dictatorship which has been established since the book was written, proves the fallacy of this assumption.

Referring further to the author of "Philip Dru: Administrator," the publisher stated: "His story shows how the seething, radical elements in the political cask today, under pressure of rising prices for the poor and greater privileges for the poor and greater privileges for the rich, literally burst into one great conflict, the Second Civil War, out of which rises the figure of Philip Dru, who shapes the future of the nation."

In the pages of this occult tome the enlightened reader finds the blueprint of the American revolution, the sinister dream as dreamed by destroyers thirty-five years ago. The plot was at that time reduced to writing, promoted later under the Wilson administration and almost carried to fruition by the New Deal. It remains to be seen whether or not the American people have sufficient moral strength and spiritual resistance to break the vicious circle.

To understand the motivation of the Communist movement operating among the nations today, one must be apprised of its connection with the international banking fraternity.

During the course of an address delivered on the floor of the House of Representatives castigating the New Deal, in June 1932, Congressman Louis T. McFadden said these words:

"Those bankers took money out of this Country to finance Japan in a war against Russia. They created a reign of terror in Russia with our money in order to help the war along. They instigated the separate peace between Germany and Russia and thus drove a wedge btween the Allies in the (first) world war. They financed Trotsky's mass meetings of discontent and rebellion in New York. They paid Trotsky's passage from New York to Russia so that he might assist in the destruction of the Russian Empire. They fomented and instigated the Russian revolution and they placed a large fund of American dollars at Trotsky's disposal in one of their branch banks in Sweden, so that through him, Russian homes might be broken up and Russian children flung far and wide from their natural protectors. They have since begun the breaking up of America."

Attacking the American System

"PHILIP DRU: ADMINISTRATOR," was written in code. As far as can be learned, it was never intended for general distribution.

An uninitiated person, reading the book for the first time, will regard it as only a work of fiction, a mediocre novel of limited reader interest. But one who understands the delphic language of the international conspirators finds in its pages a message of consuming importance involving the very soul and destiny of the United States.

Written in 1912, the author professes to be looking into the future and opens the story with the following prophetic approach: "In the year 1920, the student and the statesman saw many indications that the social, financial and industrial troubles that had vexed the United States for so long a time were about to culminate in civil war."

Then he proceeds to indict the American system of government and blame it for all the troubles to which humanity is heir. Property rights are attacked on the third page. Thereupon the hero, Philip Dru, a student just graduating from West Point is introduced.

Addressing a young lady, the daughter of a wealthy family, Dru's first words in the book are devoted to praise for the French Revolution: "Gloria, we are entering a new era." It will be shown later that this piece of literature was made the basis, the textbook, of the Roosevelt Administration. These two words "new era" became the seed thought from which the term "New Deal" sprang.

"The past is no longer to be a guide to the future," Dru continues. "A century and a half ago there arose in France a giant that had slumbered for untold centuries. . . So when he awoke he could only destroy. Unfortunately for him, there was not one of the governing class (in France) who was big enough and human enough to lend a guiding and a friendly hand, so he was led by weak and selfish men who could only incite him to further wanton murder and demolition.

"But out of that revelry of blood there dawned upon mankind the hope of a more splendid day. The giant at last knew his strength, and with head erect, and the light of freedom in his eyes, he dared to assert the liberty, equality and fraternity of men."

Thus the French Revolution is eulogized. The writer causes his hero to demand the same treatment for the American people as that which bled Frenchmen white in the great Terror of 1789. "Nowhere in the world is wealth more defiant, and monoply more insistent than in this mighty republic, and it is here that the next great battle for human emancipation will be fought and won."

The philosophy expounded in these pages ignores that under the system of free enterprise every industrious person has an opportunity equal to his fellows, for acquiring earthly possessions. This is proved by the fact of so many people in humble walks of life, born amid poverty and adversity, rising to heights and becoming independently rich.

If men, like the author of this book were sincere and altruistic, their words would sound less metallic. But in the light of the suffering that resulted from the French Revolution, not to mention the serfdom of the Russian people, the affected humanitarianism of American Communists becomes meaningless. They aspire to revolution for the purpose of advancing themselves to power. They want to build a world empire with their group dominating the human race through terrorism and a secret spy system.

A Message in Code

THE AUTHOR keeps his chief character talking: "Their (believers in the American way of life) very excesses in cruelty finally caused a revolution in feeling, and there was evolved the Christian religion of today, a religion almost wholly selfish and concerned almost entirely in the betterment of life after death . . . Socialism as dreamed of by Karl Marx cannot be entirely brought about by the leveling of wealth. If that were done without a spiritual leveling, the result would be largely as you suggest."

By this time, Philip Dru has declared himself a supporter of the doctrines that precipitated the French Revolution, and an admirer of Karl Marx. After traveling for a time in various parts of the country, he decides to make his home with the Levinskys in the Jewish section of New York City. "The thin, sharp-featured Jew and his fat, homely wife who kept it had lived in that neighborhood for many years, and Philip found them a mine of useful information . . . Ben Levinsky's forebears had long lived in Warsaw."

Since it would be impossible to inflame passions to the point of revolutionary violence without stirring Jewry, the author vividly pictures a pogrom starting at New York City, in which many lives are lost and much property destroyed. Philip Dru carries with him the spirit and ideas absorbed while living in the East Side of New York.

He takes up writing for a financial consideration. Newspapers and magazines open their columns to him. His articles sound like Roosevelt fireside talks delivered years later. Indeed, the similarity of language suggests that the late President's radio scripts may have been edited, in large measure, from the pages of "Philip Dru: Administrator."

The author caused the following to be printed in italic type to attract the eye of the reader: "In a direct and forceful manner, he (Philip Dru) pointed out that our civilization was fundamentally wrong inasmuch as among other things, it restricted efficiency; that if society were properly organized, there would be none who were not sufficiently clothed and fed ... In his second article he incorporated the story of the Levinsky's as being fairly representative of the problem he wished to treat."

Then the author consumed several pages building up a straw man, by putting a political nonentity in the White House, by the name of Rockland. A chapter is devoted to "The Making of a President," in which "conservatives" who reject the teachings of Karl Marx are subjected to a severe drubbing. Only men with bloody hands are truly virtuous!

Finally a United States Senator and the Governor of a Middle Western State meet by appointment in a hotel room. The name of the hotel is the "Mandell House."

One person reading the book sees in this name merely a place where transients eat and sleep. But another person, capable of reading between the lines and ferreting out the code message, discovers the name of the author.

"Philip Dru: Administrator" was written by the mystery man of the first world war, Colonel E. Mandell House, aptly called at the nation's capital, "the holy monk of the Wilson Administration." Wilson had the habit of referring to him as an alter ego. House admitted authorship of the book in later years. Congressman McFadden and others have charged that he was one of the inner circle responsible for the break-down of the Czar's government and rise of the Communist movement in its modern form.

Why Wilson Broke With House

BECAUSE OF THE STRANGE POWER that Mandell House exercised over Woodrow Wilson he came to be regarded as the most powerful individual in the world during the war of 1914 to 1918. The Encyclopaedia Britannica says: "Following his custom House refused any office politically as well as personally. He remained closer to the president than any member of the official family. It was upon his recommendation that Wilson chose a number of his Cabinet; after the inauguration both President and Cabinet utilized his wide knowledge of men and his shrewd estimate of political effects to help them in meeting legislative influence in the framing of the Federal Reserve Act and also played an important part in the organization of the original Federal Reserve Board. Wilson spoke of him as his 'independent self'."

After the war, Wilson fought to have the new Bolshevik government of Russia recognized, but the people of the United States refused to support him. This caused House a great deal of discomfort.

H. Wickham Steed, editor of the London Times, tells in his book, "Through Thirty Years," of Wilson's failure to gain support for Russia. He advised House to tell the President to let the matter drop. Mr. Steed adds:

"I insisted that unknown to him the prime movers were Jacob Schiff, Warburg and other international financiers who wished above all to bolster the Jewish Bolshevists to secure a field from German and Jewish exploitation of Russia."

Professor Denis Fahey of Dublin, Ireland, says in his book, "The Mystical Body of Christ in the Modern World": "According to the data furnished by the Soviet press, out of 556 important functionaries of the Bolshevik state, there were in 1918-1919, 17 Russians, 2 Ukranians, 11 Armenians, 35 Letts, 15 Germans, 1 Hungarian, 10 Georgians, 3 Poles, 3 Finns, 1 Karaim, 457 Jews."

The "Universal Jewish Encyclopedia" says: "Individual revolutionary leaders of Jewish origin played a conspicuous part in the revolution of November 1917, which enabled the Bolsheviks to take possession of the state apparatus."

Wilson's tragic mistake in trying to use his tremendous powers to foster international Communism becomes understandable by reading "Philip Dru: Administrator." Turning to page 276 of the book, the reader finds these words, written more than a decade before the Russian Revolution: "Sometimes in his day dreams, Dru thought of Russia in its vastness, of the ignorance and hopeless outlook of the people, and wondered when her deliverance would come. There was, he knew, great work for someone to do in that despotic land."

House rises to flights of eloquence as he prepares his hero for the task of giving our nation a blood bath: "Take heart, therefore, you who had lost faith in the ultimate destiny of the Republic, for a greater than Selwyn is here to espouse your cause. He comes panoplied in justice and with the light of reason in his eyes. He comes as the advocate of equal opportunity and he comes with the power to enforce his will." The next chapter bears the title, "Exultant Conspirators."

When Wilson finally realized how a net had been woven

about him, he broke with House. He gave instructions that the conspirator should never again be allowed to enter his presence. He issued a second order that House be forbidden to attend his funeral. Both wishes were faithfully observed.

Congressman McFadden stated: "It has been said that when he (Wilson) discovered the manner in which he had been misled by Colonel House, he turned against that busybody, that 'holy monk' of the financial empire, and showed him the door. He had the grace to do that, and in my opinion he deserves great credit for it."

After Wilson's death, House caused his "Intimate Papers" to be published, claiming credit for countless acts of the Administration which he secretly controlled. He later described his deceased partner as having been constitutionally unsuited for the role outlined in "Philip Dru: Administrator." About the same time he began championing Franklin Roosevelt as the "ideal President."

It will be recalled that Roosevelt went by plane from New York to the Democratic convention in Chicago and delivered an acceptance speech immediately after his first nomination to the Presidency. He flew the next day to Massachusetts to be the guest of Mandell House.

Two months after the election of Roosevelt, House published an article in Liberty Magazine entitled: "Does the United States Need a Dictator: A Warning to Selfish Capitalism, etc." In this article he admitted the authorship of Philip Dru and pointed out that the book had foreshadowed Mussolini, Hitler and Fascism by many years. Two years later in another magazine, he advocated a "New Deal for the Nations," and in Liberty Magazine, April 2, 1938, there appeared another article over his name, in which he stated that Roosevelt was accepting advice from him which Wilson had rejected. He said Roosevelt was committed to principles precious to his heart.

The New York Journal said, March 28, 1938: "After House had published his book, 'What Really Happened In Paris,' he was denounced by Senator Kenneth McKellar of Tennessee, as a 'bootlicker' who had wormed his way into the confidence of the great man, Woodrow Wilson. In 1936 Congressman George H. Tinkham suddenly began demanding an investigation of House's activities in the World War. He charged that House 'held in contempt, if not hatred, the American Constitution, the American traditions and the American form of government. Colonel House did not bother to answer either attack'."

These disclosures explain why Roosevelt established diplomatic relations with Soviet Russia less than nine months after being elected to the Presidency.

William La Varra, writing in the "American Legion Magazine," said: "For fifteen deceitful years the corrupt Kremlin had tried to obtain a communist base, protected by diplomatic immunities within the United States; four Presidents — Wilson, Harding, Coolidge and Hoover — had refused to countenance Moscow's pagan ideology or its carriers. But here, at last, was a President the communists could deal with."

The Great American Massacre

MANDELL HOUSE visualized civil war for the United States. The fact that it did not materialize in his lifetime was no doubt another disappointment to him.

His book looked forward to a time when "the whole social and industrial fabric of the nation was at high tension needing but a spark to explode."

"Men at once divided themselves into groups," says the author. "A mass meeting was called to take place the day following in New York's largest public hall.

"The hall was packed to its limits an hour before the time named. A distinguished college president from a nearby town was given the chair, and in a few words he voiced the indignation and the humiliation which they all felt. Then one speaker after another bitterly denounced the administration, and advocated the overthrow of the government. One more intemperate than the rest, urged an immediate attack on Thor and all his kind. This was met by a roar of approval."

House used all the literary arts of which he was capable to put the American government in a bad light. Only deceivers can win politically and govern a nation under a representative system. Dictators alone make honest and capable leaders, according to House.

Philip Dru being in the crowd, fights his way to the stage, gives his name to the chairman, and asks to be heard.

The mob immediately yields to his oratory and comes under his control.

The revolution is on! Dru has been secretly training a labor army for combat. Thousands of men use wooden guns in drilling, but are equipped with real rifles and an abundance of ammunition in their homes. The first skirmish of the war takes place in Wisconsin during the month of September, but the struggle soon spreads over the entire eastern half of the United States. The South refuses to take sides either way.

Resorting to the vernacular of the Apocalypse, House places his mythical figure on the back of a beautiful charger: "In that hell storm of lead and steel Dru sat upon his horse unmoved. With bared head and eyes aflame, with face flushed and exultant, he looked the embodiment of the terrible god of war.

"Dru's soldiers saw that victory was theirs, and maddened by the lust of war, they drove the Government forces back, killing and crushing the seething and helpless mass that was now in hopeless confusion."

Dru with four hundred thousand men, beats the regular army of six hundred thousand to its knees. He has been amply supplied with funds through the cooperation of certain international bankers. Thereupon a significant code message drops from his lips: "I feel already as if my name were written high upon the walls of my country's Valhalla."

News of Dru's momentous victory quickly circles the globe. He is pictured as walking amid the ruins of what was once a peaceful and prosperous nation. House says: "They recognized the fact that Dru dominated the situation and that a master mind had at last arisen in the Republic." Dictatorship was officially inaugurated on American soil. The Constitution of the United States was abolished. Human liberty was at an end. Dru chose for himself the title, "Administrator of the Republic."

"It was felt that the property and lives of all were now in the keeping of one man."

Dru's first public utterance after the revolution bears a strange resemblance to the language with which the American people became accustomed in Franklin Roosevelt's fireside talks: "We all agree that a change had to be brought about even though it meant revolution, for otherwise the cruel hand of avarice would have crushed out from us, and from our children, every semblance of freedom."

Thereupon Dru struck where Roosevelt later delivered his most powerful blow, namely, at the United States Supreme Court. This becomes understandable because the New Deal was, from its inception, geared according to the Philip Dru pattern. Moreover, dictatorship cannot countenance law. It is essentially lawless.

In the last analysis there are only two kinds of government—government by men and government by law. Totalitarianism supplants the latter with the former. House devotes a whole chapter to "The Reform of the Judiciary."

Dru brings the judicial branch of the government under his personal control. The same was true with regards to the

Congress. Men serving in both branches become puppets dominated by the "master mind." Dru swayed the masses of people with his oratory to such an extent that they applauded the loss of their liberties.

Franklin Roosevelt and the group that came to power with him used the Philip Dru code as a guide undermining the government. Plots toward this end were constantly hatched in White House circles.

America in Danger

SPEAKING BEFORE the Rotary Club at Detroit, Michigan, on June 27, 1934 James Farley referred to Roosevelt as follows: "The President's head is cool and his feet are on the ground. His plan was worked out for him before he was nominated."

When Roosevelt felt especially good, playful and pleased over the way things were going he would say to Washington associates and newspaper men: "We planned it that way."

An old-time representative of the press at Washington says that the remark always created an awkward situation because the hearers knew they were "in the presence of an unsolved mystery." No one knew for sure who was meant by the use of the word "We."

After the revolution Philip Dru worked out what the book describes as "A New Code of Laws."

Every essential phase of the Roosevelt legislative program will be found in this section. The White House planners obviously used it as a text for drawing up the many alphabetical revolutionary measures that proved so distasteful to loyal Americans during the years of New Deal blight.

Roosevelt said the Constitution was an instrument to be relegated to the "days of the horse and buggy." Philip Dru said that the document was satisfactory "for the first hundred years of our existence, but under the conditions of today it is not only obsolete, but even grotesque."

Under Roosevelt the so-called "lame duck" session of Congress was abolished. Philip Dru said: "Our House of Representatives is supposed to be our popular lawmaking body, and yet its members do not convene until a year and one month from the time they are elected."

The New Deal administration enacted legislation so that the government would make extensive loans of money directly to the people. Philip Dru said: "I am also planning to inaugurate cooperative loan societies in every part of the Union and I have appointed a commissioner to instruct the people as to their formation and conduct and to explain their beneficial results."

Instead of helping the citizens to become self-reliant, Roosevelt made them feel directly responsible to the government by obligating them through a coercive plan. Philip Dru said: "Under my personal direction I am having prepared an old-age pension law and also a laborers' insurance law, covering loss in case of illness, incapacity and death."

Under the New Deal the WPA became a national scandal. Philip Dru said: "And if no work is to be had, I shall arrange that every indigent person that is honest and industrious shall be given employment by the Federal, State, County or Municipal Government as the case may be."

Wage and hour legislation was introduced by the New Deal. Philip Dru said: "Furthermore, it shall in the future be unlawful for any employer of labor to require more than eight hours work a day, and then for only six days a week. If an attempt is made to reduce wages by shortening hours or for any other cause, the employe shall have the right to go before the magistrate and demand that the amount of wage be adjusted there."

The specter of socialized medicine began to haunt the medical profession during the era of Roosevelt misrule and exploitation. Philip Dru said: "There is another matter to which I shall give my earnest attention and that is the reformation of the study and practice of medicine ... A large part of our medical schools and colleges are entirely unfit for the purposes intended, and each year they grant diplomas to hundreds of ignorant young men and women and license them to prey upon a more or less helpless people. The number of physicians per inhabitant is already ridiculously large, many times more than is needful, or than other countries where the average of the professions ranks higher, deem necessary."

Roosevelt made a desperate effort to have the government take over telegraph, telephone and other systems of communication. Philip Dru said: "Certain of the public corporations should be taken over bodily by the National Government and accordingly the Postmaster General was instructed to negotiate with the telegraph and telephone companies for their properties at a fair valuation."

During the Roosevelt regime there was a scandal regarding his attempt to abolish holding companies. The book says: "The Administrator insisted upon the prohibition of franchise to 'holding companies' of whatsoever character. In the past, he declared, they have been prolific trust breeders, and those existing at that time, he asserted, should be dissolved."

Roosevelt's personal hatred for State Rights became well known because this doctrine, advocated by our founding fathers, stood in the way of his scheme for making the entire nation directly responsible to the central government at Washington. The book says: "Dru's father had been an ardent advocate of State rights, and the Administrator had been reared in that atmosphere; but when he began to think out such questions for himself, he realized for himself that density of population and rapid inter-communication afforded by electric and steam railroads, motors, aeroplanes, telephones were, to all practical purposes, obliterating State lines and molding the country into a homogeneous nation. Therefore, after the Revolution, Dru saw that the time had come for this trend to assume more definite form, and for the National Government to take upon itself some of the functions heretofore exclusively within the jurisdiction of the States."

The foregoing parallelism between Roosevelt's policies and Philip Dru's utterances does not profess to be complete. Only a meager summation is here presented. The analogy can be traced almost indefinitely.

Even a casual reading of phrases put into Dru's mouth by Mandell House, show where Roosevelt and his crew of ghost writers got many of their ideas and terms used over the radio and otherwise. Turning through the pages of the book promiscuously one comes upon the following passages with a familiar ring:

"My fellow countrymen, I feel sure that however much we may differ as to methods, there is no one within the sound of my voice who does not wish me well.

"The policy of this government is that every man or woman who desires work shall have it, even if the government has to give it.

"I shall arrange that every indigent person that is honest and industrious shall be given employment by the Federal, State, County or Municipal government.

"I wish it also understood that an adequate wage must be paid for labor. Labor is no longer to be classed as an inert commodity to be bought and sold by the law of supply and demand.

"Where there are a large number of employees affected, they can act through their unions or societies. This law shall be applicable to women as well as to men.

"Under my personal direction I am having prepared an old age pension law and also a laborers' insurance law, covering losses in case of illness, incapacity and death.

"I have a commission working on an efficient coopera-tive system of marketing the products of small farms and factories.

"I am also planning to inaugurate cooperative loan so-cieties in every part of the Union.

"The Supreme Court is ever present with its Damoclean sword. It is nearly impossible for the desires of our people to find expression into a law."

Mandell House caused his hero to bring leaders of the governmental bureaucracy together for frequent informal discussions, and such occasions were called "FIRESIDE TALKS"—according to page 254 of the book.

The Code Meaning of Philip Dru

A N ATTORNEY in California who has had considerable experience in code breakdown, finds the title "Philip Dru: Administrator" to be revealing. He says there can be no doubt as to its cabalistic origin.

His starting point is Philip of Macedon, the father of Alexander the Great, who devoted his life to acquisition of power over Greece and the education of his son for its use as a means toward bringing the entire world into subjection. Philip conquered by bribery, for which he is historically infamous. The very term "philippize" means to gain power through bribery.

According to the attorney's theory, the symbol *Dru* stands for David Rex Universal, or David Rex of the Universe — David king over all.

Kings are designated by initials. GRB, George Rex Britain. LRF, Louis Rex France. Initials thus appropriated are engraved on the royal seal, the coat of arms, the royal coach and otherwise displayed. All countries have followed this custom.

The name most likely to be chosen by international Jewish leaders would be David, since in their spiritual blindness they pose as possessors of his Old Testament kingdom on earth. Every informed person is familiar with their aspirations for complete domination of the human race.

Most surely the second initial, "R," would be for Rex, says the attorney. This leaves the third letter to stand for one thing, the Universe or Universal.

He summarizes as follows: Philip of Macedon was noted as an Administrator. Ability to give Greece a good administration aided him in attaining his objectives via the road of bribery.

The deliberate and malicious plan of the New Deal was from its inception, to destroy liberty by bribing the electorate. Farmers, as an example, were asked to sell their souls by accepting AAA benefits.

Philip's personality and methods were chosen to symbolize the program organized ultimately to install the world emperor David Rex Universal — Philip Dru: Administrator.

★   ★   ★

THE FACTS presented in this chapter were known to me several years before Franklin Roosevelt was publicly suggested as an aspirant to the White House. His collaboration with Mandell House and other members of the group committed to the task of destroying America, was known to me more than a year before he received the Presidential nomination the first time.

I had no choice but make the truth known as a service to the Church of Jesus Christ and the Country we love. This has caused me to be singled out for a great deal of persecution. Orders were finally given by the White House to silence my voice and destroy our religious and patriotic labors.

Our exposures proved annoying to conspirators.

The United States is facing its supreme test. The success or failure of the nation in resisting the forces of destruction will be determined by the strength or weakness of the Cause of Christ in this part of the world. The Christian Gospel faithfully proclaimed will build national character and strengthen soul muscle for triumph over these powers of darkness. There is no other hope.

www.ingramcontent.com/pod-product-compliance
Lightning Source LLC
Chambersburg PA
CBHW071106090426
42737CB00013B/2503